God Loves His People

written by Tiffany Thomas
illustrated by Nikki Casassa

CFI • An imprint of Cedar Fort, Inc. • Springville, Utah

HARD WORDS:
people, lead, follow

PARENT TIP: "sh" can be difficult for younger children to pronounce. Allow them to develop at their own pace for a little bit.

God loves
His people.

He sends men to lead
them in His ways.

3

Lehi and Nephi are
some of these men.

So are Mosiah, Helaman, Mormon, and Moroni.

The men love God and Jesus (and their people).

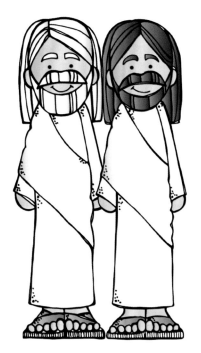

They follow Jesus.

They show how to have
faith and do good.

We can have faith and do good.

We can be like these men of God.

We can be like Jesus, too.

God loves us and we love Him.

The end.

This is not an official publication of The Church of Jesus Christ of Latter-day Saints. The opinions and views expressed herein belong solely to the author and do not necessarily represent the opinions or views of Cedar Fort, Inc. Permission for the use of sources, graphics, and photos is also solely the responsibility of the author.

ISBN 13: 978-1-4621-4337-5

Published by CFI, an imprint of Cedar Fort, Inc. • 2373 W. 700 S., Suite 100, Springville, UT 84663
Distributed by Cedar Fort, Inc., www.cedarfort.com

Cover design and interior layout design by Shawnda T. Craig
Cover design © 2022 Cedar Fort, Inc.
Printed in China • Printed on acid-free paper
10 9 8 7 6 5 4 3 2 1